What I

Poems by

Iris Litt

SHIVASTAN Publishing

TABLE OF CONTENTS

Caterpillars

You wanted me to kill
the caterpillars who fell
from the eaves to the floor
of the porch, but I said No
and left for New York

and when I came back
I found only the skins
they had left behind
that looked like death

but a waft of air
(a caterpillar soul?)
flew near my ear
and told me where
to look: around, all around
the flowerbeds, the lawn.
I think it was my reward.
I looked to the green
where some flew free
free, bright and alive
free of that dark disguise.
I had found them
living as butterflies.

Sunspot

Through the circular pane
I see that today
our plane is not
a dark shadow
but a bright sunspot
on the land
I don't know why
maybe the sun
in a cloud-free sky
bouncing off the silver belly
turns silver to gold
and beams it to earth
as a golden coin
that travels with us
on fields, lagoons, the sea

like some bright other self
the sun-gladdened undamaged self of us
that precedes us always
like a machete that cuts a swath
through the jungle
or a smile that clears a path
through the crowd.

Flight 261

You probably packed as I'm doing today,
decided to take the long blue flowered dress
in case something dressy came up,
left the shampoo behind; you'd buy some.
Did the whole packing dance:
you'd take that one book,
the computer disk with your life's work,
the white sandals.

Decisions, decisions,
but you felt you'd done well,
were well-prepared for the life
in the sun

but this one
was a decision you couldn't make:
the huge plane spiraled out of control
smashed the water right off the
very beach I'm headed for.

You could control the blue dress
but not the instant
shortly after you left Vallarta
when you left yourself
and became part of
the blue water.

Losing it

I'm losing it, you said.
Sight. Hearing. Mind.
And I thought: At the start
you didn't have it to lose.
Couldn't see farther than a nipple
couldn't say a word
or recognize a sound
could only tell gentle from loud, siren from song.
So it was only yours to use
not to lose, not to keep
and you can return it like you would a library book
when you're going to be moving away.
Try being born again
before sight, hearing, mind,
be helpless, laugh, be cute again
satisfied and fat after feeding
unashamed to ask for a lullaby
or smile a dumb smile.
Don't fight losing it
in fact don't lose it
but with the graciousness
this long day has taught you
give it up.

Numbering the days

They say her days are numbered
and I wonder, does she do her math
each morning, swing her legs
over the side of the bed
stick her feet out for her scuffs
recite Day Sixty-four and the door shuts
at ninety. Three months
and the days go, so smoothly, so fast
one morning she will have counted to ninety
her last, give or take a few.
And I wonder, I wonder
can you try to un-number your days?
can you play Counting Backwards
and do you repeat all the wise poetic clichés?
The moving finger writes and having writ moves on.
Take your place on the great mandala. Approach thy couch
as one who... lies down to pleasant dreams.
Rage, rage against the dying of the light.

The clichés are trying to say: there is no way out.
Sixty-eight. Seventy-three.
Put your feet in your scuffs and keep your count
and when your number is called
answer, I'll be right out.

What I wanted to say

I wanted to say:
I got all dressed up
like a Barbie doll
who says Yes when you
wind her up.

But I said:
I think
I'll fix you
another drink.

I wanted to say:
Love me, please love me
or go away

but I said:
A funny thing happened today
in the Grand
Union.

I said:
I'd like to have a word...
and you said
I'm sure you would
but when I did,
you did not like
what you heard.

There is no way
to reconcile
what I wanted to say
and what I said
instead.

Life

After plenty trouble and sweat
I thought all
would be vindicated
by a perfect well almost
love
happy grown children
independent income
freedom to travel the world
my mind eternally young
in my voluptuously aging body
wearing its hip young clothes

well
here it is
you
driving me crazy
too much to do
while adding to
my shrinking purse

and life
it doesn't think
it owes me a thing

not a friend
life accepts
my courage ingenuity work
matter of fact

and says
button your lip
and keep plugging
till the end

Without anaesthetic

The root canal dentist said
I do it without anaesthetic
so you can tell me
if the nerve is alive.

Of course, I said. We have to
get to the root of this
thinking myself brave and clever,
thinking, sooner or later
this will be over, and
did anyone ever die in a dentist's chair?

When I leapt upward
we both said
The nerve is alive
though not well

and he gave me my shot

and I said
I guess being alive
means pain
so we need
every shot
we can get.

The symbol

Some cookies in the freezer
got old, ice-burned, and turned
to mold

and I learned
that the cookies
weren't just cookies to you.
They were cheap, you said, bright pink
and they made you think how
gaudy and cheap it all is

but I remembered my tenderness
as I paid the blank-faced clerk
at Rite-Aide the dollar forty-nine
and I had walked two extra blocks
for sugarless strawberry cream,
ridiculously, happily pink

so I froze them
and in the cold they mutated
into some creature alive with mold.

Then you turned your rage on me
for buying your cookies cheap
and frozen and strawberry

and I cried, thinking of how
I had tried to please you, and we agreed
you should move out

because the ice had burned the cookies
and your rage had turned me
into an angry, whimpering thing
and the cookies weren't just cookies
they were symbols and nothing
would ever be the same again.

Messenger

You'd think the radio, the internet, the TV
the newspaper, the cellphone, the movies
could tell all these people
who escaped the cold
how it was

but nothing tells like the human mouth
the flicker of eye
the body miming
a shovelling move
a snowshoeing glide

so it was that I became
the courier of old
the messenger from afar
whether brought by horse or plane.
Now after my long journey
I look into their eager eyes,
am plied with cold drinks, hot tea,
pled to tell them specifically

how the great snowstorm was
how the dense snow fell at three inches per hour
fell for twelve hours without pause
buried our regrets, anger, loss
buried us so we could arise
brand new.
Like the TV, the internet, the New York Times, I try
to tell them. To really tell them
I'll need a poem.

A death

It's only autumn
but the college says
to make my teaching plan
for April, May and June.
She can't make a plan.
What she has lost
is time

while I still have an April
May and June
and on and on.
Why have her cells turned on her
while mine gallop happily along?
She has lost
but I have won
this fall day
when the sun
illuminates the red and gold leaves
and a sky of ferocious blue.

She has lost the leaves, the air
the joy, the sky
the month, the year
lost the fight, lost all
to a stupid cell
and no one knows why.

In the park

In the park
in New York
I saw a little white dog
with three legs
whose owner walked too fast
so the little dog
kept sitting down to rest
but the owner wouldn't stop
and the dog hopped
the best he could

and I saw a handsome young man
with a graying beard
whom I had seen before
wheel into the park in his chair
who had lost his leg
and unlike the dog
had only one left

and I was struck
with a sorrow so deep
I left the park
on my strong legs.

The way machines die

Machines die instantaneously
with no apology.
They may moan or shriek a bit
squeak or squeal or emit a little
death rattle

but they do not accuse you
nor make excuses for you.
If you think it happened because
you worked them too hard
were too busy to oil them
were rough with them
or simply didn't love them enough
don't worry because

machines die the way we should,
simply and without regret.
We know their estimated life span
(they come with manuals)
but every time, it's still too soon.
It is always we, the survivors,
who aren't ready yet.

Nothing happened

Nothing happened, I told my friends.
As the personal ads would describe it:
You, handsome male artist living in Stockholm
and I, American female living in New York

met on the nude beach, the plati, in Patmos
you with a blonde German goddess
I with a distinguished Greek statesman

both of whom obligingly disappeared
(with each other, for that matter)
as those gossipy Greek gods had ordained

so we shared a room in Mykonos
and in a moment of awkwardness
before we undressed
you said, oh well, after all, we met on the nude beach
and I said, in fact I hardly recognize you
                              with your clothes on
and we laughed, took them off
and fell into our respective beds

then for three days walked the ancient narrow streets
of this Cycladian island
your arm over my shoulder
my arm around your waist
and sat on a rock under an olive tree
where you told me about you
and I told you about me

nothing happened, I tell you,
but that's a lie
what happened was rare:
a taste of absolute joy.

Inheritance of stars

On Halloween she came to my party
as a Berber queen
dark skin black wig
and between the eyes and brows
tiny silver stars

which floated from her skin to earth
so that after she went home
I found an inheritance of stars.
Stars danced on my rug
winked from the indigo spread

and when I looked out
from under my stoop
the three steps up
were littered with stars.

Stars

I procrastinate
because I'd hate to vacuum up
the tiny tinsel fallen stars
that floated from her Halloween face
to my rug, my sill
my basement stair.
She wants to be found
and if you want to find her
just follow her trail of stars
as she walks across town
to her East Village.
When she left my house
she left to me
a sprinkling of this galaxy of stars.
They startle me
every time they catch the light
and beam their silver fire my way.
Before they came
my nights were dark
as all nights are
without the stars.

Waiting tables at
the Mama Buddha Café

The plump statue of Papa Buddha
was looking the other way
when the boss refused to pay off
the building inspector
and that closed the sidewalk café.
But inside, the young women still peel,
                              chip and chirp.
Their greens are fresh, their spices are perfect.
Do they worship the Mama Buddha?
Do they sleep in bunks?
Are they bonded servants?
Are they the little Chinese girls
who would have been thrown into the river
before girlbabies proved salable
to American couples who waited too long
to be fertile?
Now, smiling and proud
they earn their saved lives.
Papa Buddha is fat
but the girls are very thin.
They remember the river, the mud
                              of huts and roads.
They remember the stories of the mothers.

Futureroots

The futureshock world
of new and used bodyparts
new electronically-powered plastic arms,
                                    legs and hearts
has led to a new occupation among the old
that didn't exist with carried milk pails,
                                    ten children and wagons west
a game old people play on themselves
like a beloved automobile
replacing, checking, polishing up parts
bravely bearing the soldering, cutting and stitching.

All right, I will be such an old person,
                                give up being vain
this mannequin self that turns and sucks in
                                    cheeks before mirrors
on one condition: that that reconstructed
                                edifice be built around
this wacky brain
that forever steers me to an unfindable
                        old farmhouse
within sound of water and woods still wild
a poor inflexible humanoid rejecting space
and struggling to root its plastic feet in earth.

Anna's sign

Here signs remain
far beyond the time
of those they name.
No one wants to be the one to take them down.
It would be like a voodoo wish of further death,
a little killing, an act of rejection, a denial of memory
and someone might do the same to me.
You know Old Anna down the road
with the neat white hair, drawn back like mine,
well, Anna died. I don't mind
thinking I hear her light step
in the road nor seeing her slight figure
in the mist as she walks her small white dog
and I'm resigned to seeing no light at night;
her window was the only one I saw
and it left me to be the only pinpoint
in this blackness of woods
every 10:30, anyhow until that final one.
I don't really mind.
I'm just wondering who will remove the sign.
But the tall weeds she fought climb
over it. The violent mountain storms
                                try to wash it away.
The cruel mountain frosts try to split it.
We will wait
and in her lifetime's length or less
Anna's sign
will be removed
by Time.

The woodstove

I'm good with wood
but this wood is hard
hard to start
resists the fire.
At first I'm annoyed
but it reminds me I've had
paper fires, fastwood fires
that quickly flickered out
and then it shows me
it's the kind of wood
that, once caught,
will burn long and steady and merry
so it's worth the wait
and that's the kind of fire I want.

I pray to the god "Recycle"

I make these offerings
to the god "Recycle"
in a sky-blue plastic bag:
kleenex boxes, vodka bottles, foil

and hang up a clear bag
for deposit bottles:
ginger ale, tonic, beer
that the pilgrimage of poor
can get a nickel for.

I pray to the god "Recycle"
as I pray to Chacmool for rain.
My offerings to him include:
the blood of the lamb on the meat wrapper
the crumbs in the cardboard cookie box
and pieces of me on the kleenex and paper towels:
my hair, my nails, my blood, my tears
and the paper.
crumpled paper, straight paper
old poems and shopping lists
I add to the paper of millions like me

so some day
in one of the gigantic meadows
which we may have saved
which may still exist

we can build a mile-high bonfire
and dance around it
when the moon is full.

The blue plastic bag

Always the old things
have called out to me from the curb,
the backless chair I rename a stool,
the piece of picket fence
I seek a space in my fence for.

I save them the way
I save lost words

but I am not the sea
and if I were
I would be filling up.

Now in this bag
blue as the sea
I place this piece of string
which might turn out to be the prize
in the popcorn box of my planet.

On passing my old office building
on the Madison Avenue bus

Every day for thirty years
I went into that mine
in which the elevator went up
not down

it was a word-mine
in which I dug
for words that sell
yet between the writings
of those clever lines

poetry poured from me
poured like light
from eyes, skin, mind

so bright
that my boss saw it
sensed the poems
and sent me home.

Epitaph for the Twin Towers

We called you ugly
said you looked like
giant tombstones
and then you were.

We called you too big
but you had to be
since you were tombstones
for thousands.

We thought you were ugly and too big
but because of the way you died

we walk south now
on every avenue
look down at our feet
try not to see
at the end of the street
the empty sky.

Six months after

Such a warm winter
since September
the trees budding
early and eager
so I picture the Towers
waking like tulips
just two more flowers
growing again
after their sleeping
September to March
like the New York ailanthus
that dares to grow
with its roots in rubble
and concrete and blackness
into great trees.

Like a photo growing
on my screen
the Towers sprout
the windows fill in
and finally
the people come back
talking and laughing
nonchalantly
enjoying the view.

Then I jolt awake and say,
these are not perennials.
The flowers were asleep
but the Towers and their humans
are borne away forever on the wind
perennial only
in the mind.

The Gypsy children

When my purse disappeared
from under the table
in the sidewalk cafe
in Firenze

everyone said:
It's the Gypsy children
again.

Since no head showed
above the table
you're under three feet high
and probably no more than four years old,
small for your age,
poor nutrition.

But your skill, your brain
are greater than mine

and so is your need.
I hope when you brought them my purse
they gave you food.

Lost in Firenze

The *polizia* asked me
to list what I'd lost.
My dollars, my lire,
my checks, my passport,
kleenex, address book and more,
and yes, my Italian phrasebook
but at least I already knew
how to shout
Polizia, aiuta, help

and at least I had left in my room
my plane ticket
Firenze to Rome
Rome to New York
so I still had the best thing
you or I could have:
a ticket to home.

GypsyGap

There was a Gap gift card
in that wallet
the Gypsy Kid stole
in Firenze;

the gift card is good at
Gap, GapKids, BabyGap

and I picture the ragged GypsyKid
transformed into a GapKid
and on his/her back,
a Gap knapsack
to carry stolen loot
and Gap sandals
on the bare brown feet

and I wish I'd had
a gift card
from Dean & Deluca or Fauchon
or whatever's chic in Firenze

so the GypsyGap kid
could shop for
something to eat.

The nursing home

My mother arrived
in my vintage convertible
with the top open
under a bright sky
the sun on her face.

My mother left
in the dark
in a box
with no wheels
the top closed.

Morning coffee

My mother sold her life
for Coffee Insurance:
A lifetime guarantee
of coffee
brought to her
hot and fresh each morning.

My mother went to this place
where they bring it to your room.
No need to measure into the spoon
boil and pour as she had done
for over ninety years,
no more stumbling around the kitchen
unable to clearly see
the dirt on the stove
or the room's disarray.

I said she'd be better off
in her peaceful kitchen
but she wouldn't listen
and she had her coffee.
Here's the irony:
A full cup of bitterness
with free refills
served by quick impersonal hands
below a hostile face

so she started each day
with a strong and bitter blend
diluted by her tears.

A small boat

She folded her hands over her chest
as though saying Ready For Death

and as I leaned over her
I heard the sea in her
sloshing through her lungs
the tide rising and falling inside.

My mother was a small boat
that had shipped water
after ninety-two sturdy years
of cresting all waves

even though she was a boat
crafted in Kansas
the land of no-sea
where she crested waves of grain.

Her brain lived on
for four waterlogged months
a creature of the deep
until her drowning was complete.

The calendar

My mother asked me for a calendar
that didn't cost anything.
She made me return
the one I'd bought.
She would only have the kind
stores gave out free.
"Well, they don't any more, mother."
"Well, they must, they always did
when I was a child."

Now a calendar has arrived
not from a store, I was right about that,
but from a wildlife group;
they'd like a donation.
I could have told her it was free
and sent the donation secretly.
The calendar even has baby animals on it
multiple births for some.
She would have loved looking at it
on her institutional wall
but it came after she had gone.

The mail order catalog

You know those things my mother asked for,
she never asked for much
but this time she asked with force

but I couldn't get them
because her catalog didn't come

I mean her mail-order book
where she got the pull-on skirts
with the elastic waist
eight dollars, washable.
I watched her mail
but her catalog never came.

Fifteen years too late,
the catalog found me.
I pick out a skirt for her,
the navy, the grey,
the herringbone would be nice,
eighteen dollars, no longer eight

and I want to call the company and ask
Where were you that terrible year
and couldn't you have sent it
while she was here
but the clerk would only say
I'm sorry, we have no record of it
and have a nice day.

MacDump

What will you do with
your letters to me
which are in your Mac's memory
if not in your own?

Will you drag me down
into your Trash Icon
called in Real Reality
a Trash Can

and dump me into
that virtual space
so no new lady
who might get into your Mac
some morning when you've
gone off to work
and left her at your place
will find a file named Iris
and virtually scroll her way
through our years?

Once your letters would have been
in a shoebox
tied with a blue ribbon.

You do as you like.
I'm tying a pink ribbon
around my Mac.

Habits

When I sew
pins slip
to the floor
where you walk bare
and shriek.

You set the alarm
and go back to sleep
while I lie awake.

You think
this is no worse
than those toothpaste globs
I leave in the sink.

You say you'll call at two
to tell me when to meet you
but you call at three
to ask if I'll be here
when you call at four
by which time
you may have
made up your mind
what to do at five.

I try to use our magic
like a pail of lime
which they say dissolves
all things including rage

so I can get to the clear
rippleless surface
of the love that lives
beneath these waves
like a fathomless pond.

Early stages

Try to remember
now is the dream part

remember you learned
heaven is not enough

try to remember ahead
the sock on the floor
the listlessness, hostility
and other realities
of the heavenly
chosen one

but by then
your heart will be trapped
like a little forest animal

who still hopes
and eagerly endures the pain
as it gnaws off
its own leg.

I know the feeling

I know the feeling.
You do good work
You're proud

and then, well, what? A snub
a nasty word
a sticky wicket
in which you're misunderstood,
unappreciated, unseen

and suddenly
you're just a little girl again
and everything you've won
is gone.
You are little and crying and alone.
Someone is leaving, someone has left,
someone isn't coming home.

The New York State Thruway

This mother of highways only warns.
Warns of things I might otherwise
have thought lovable:
intimately low bridges, fallen rock in reminiscent shapes,
soft shoulders, deer so free of fear
they cross roads. No signs say
Smooth road ahead. Fresh wind. Cloudpuffs.
Freedom ahead. A happy hour. A good poem. Sunribbon ahead
winding and coasting white-gold on green.
Say nothing of the open-car exhilaration
of the repeating moments of meeting
of sun and wind on skin.
Nor speak of clapboard farmhouses, carved iron pumps,
unfallen rock and smaller roads that turn off
to iced sodapop streams
where we splash, laugh, stretch in the sun and
sleep on the earth's tickly green mattress.

No wonder that road appears in my dreams
as a symbol of happiness. It never warns
of the real perils: loss of love,
defection of friend, trying to be good, immobility,
the belief that what you see is what you get
or simply the chronic fear of low bridges, fallen rock,
soft shoulders and deer crossings. (Even Burmashave
once caught that neurosis:
"Hardly a man is now alive
who went over this hill at seventy-five.")

No, I disagree
with the New York State Thruway. Although
on this highway I know of night and rain
each year passes and my night
does not come, only this delight
punctuated by the clean bright predictable pain
and the clear free sunribbon ahead.
The non-truth is fear.
The New York State Thruway
is only half right.

While recovering, I meet a lame pigeon

Like me
he walks unevenly
lists to the left stands on one foot
hops up the step
to the Statue of Man
as I gawk get wet-eyed
have visions of veterinarians
and I the guide
down the brave rehabilitative route

but he stands still on that foot
and looks at me
as though he can see
my noble intentions
that small eye filled with
pity for me? superiority?

and with a grand flap of wing
lifts and skims above the plaza
transcending me
as, alone again,
I limp across it
away from the grand
Statue of Man.

Flying east

Flying east
flying fast
coast to coast
out of sun and dust
into mist.
Prepare to land
circling into that dark bottom
where I live beneath the surface
three steps down
underground
in a time of deprivation

Flying east
through this mist of sight
flying east alone
with you beside me
somewhere over Texas
my tears dried up
anthropomorphically
like that land

We pass the sun
but it is going west
seems happy
leaving us behind.
It takes its light
and streaks past.
We are shedding hours
losing time
flying east
into night.

Then you extend your hand.
We descend through clouds
into dark away from sun.
Below I see eight million lights.
Together
we prepare to land.

Lunch hour in Central Park

Hot and tired at the start
I safari deeper and deeper into green
in search of What Was Once Here
welcoming the landmarks: first, grass
then a bird a squirrel water ducks
tall grass natural rock a sort of meadow
almost bare of beercans

thus progressing backward from
that windowless room where I work
in that curtainwall mountain set in smoothed-over rock
as others once struggled forward
toward that from which I retreat
a figure on a mirror-read chart of The Ascent of Man

and finally in my Backward Mobility descend to
barefoot primitive joy
for one hour.

The country of Time

Those small persons are gone.
Where did they go? They went to Time.
The five year old with the lisp, happily telling me
(please read this with a lisp):
"The school syclogist said I can come to the special speech class."
The seven-year-old explaining infinity to the five year old:
"It's whenever you get there, there's still more."
They are gone like Pacific fishing villages I have known,
not swept away in floods or leveled by earthquakes,
but simply grown, dirt paved, palapas into white concrete condos.
They've gone to a landscape in time not place
so that time itself becomes a place.
I like to think they are still somewhere there
in the country of Time
seabreeze ruffling a palapa roof inside a rigid building,
child inside man, living.

son moving

for Dean

the makeup base
was streaked all week
the black eyeliner well I left it
off   the eyebrow pencil was fine
the tears didn't go that high
the tears went deep deep down
to where you started
back to the time
I felt you kick

so this week
I leave the makeup off
and say I'll be okay
and why do I make so much of it
and anyhow so many sons do it
move away

After you moved out of
the upstairs apartment

I hear footsteps on the stair
but they're
not you, they're
indefinably lighter and they're
not coming here, they're going somewhere else.
On the other hand they do
sound like you
just enough to
make me raise my head and
listen awhile and smile.

Spring thaw

Beyond the dripping porch and falling stalactites
the meadow gradually reveals itself.
The chair we left on its side in November reappears.
The stone wall is back.

A body is discovered two miles up creek
as are the reminders of your casualness:
the car you bought in October and left under snow,
the frost-split pipe, my anger
and other forms of happiness and loss

and like the stream that now adds to its April flow
the very ice that imprisoned it all winter
your face and form add a strange new energy
to this sum of self that will soon be
greening alone in the green meadow.

Winter morning

While you still sleep
I scurry on small-animal feet
bring in firewood, start two fires
heat water, drink tea with honey
swallow kelp, light cigarettes
uncork the brandy, find my warm sweater
ponder the possible sources
of energy, heat and light
then in the warming house
wake you for love
and obsolete
all other forms
of heat.

Photo

I lost you among giant green fans
on that sand road with its snow of muleprints.

What was real
remembers like a travel folder of
postcard canals, lagoons, coconut groves
and other clichés.

Beyond the hometurning shrimp boat
in a spectacular Pacific sunset
you disappeared from my horizon

which is a geography as stubborn as any.

Here in the cold house
my camera coughs you up
and I touch your celluloid cheek

but you stay
there where you froze in the tropical sun.

I can't make peace with that peaceful lagoon

All that
blue water, green
earth, jumping fish,
doesn't mean
we'll refind, soon or later,
that same or another lagoon
with your harmonica carrying clear
to infinity.
Some places and people won't go,
they stay as though
they're from your snake or chimp life.
I try to disqualify that Eden,
remind myself that it sits happily
on a seismological fault,
that once a tidal wave
drowned 3,000 Adams-and-Eves sleeping
naked and smiling in each other's arms as we did
but all the sharks, giant manta rays
                            and scorpions on that sea or earth
can't seem to discredit those bright days
and some stubborn camera in my mind
continues to see
that earth as kind, that life, free.

Now time widens like water I float farther
the tiny blue indentation on the map
shrinks smaller than a pinpoint
as though my eyes are 4,000-mile binoculars
but are getting older
so that the first mist ever seen on that lagoon
now dims its micro-likeness.
I am lost in air as though
the plane didn't land and
how strange I can't
make peace with that peaceful lagoon:
I can't discredit it
and I can't get to it.

Letter to the tropics

The plane too big for propellers
landed smoothly among plastic and plumbing.
The face in my mirror is a negative
like your other side of the equator:
dark face framed by hair whitening with sun and time.
I am my ancestor delivered to this sleek place,
                              amiss among faucets.
I cover the sea-fragrance of my skin with perfume and,
urbane artist with sure hand,
pygmalion myself to fashion
so I can go anonymously in the crowd.
The radiator clanks jungle drums,
the grey sky fades me to monotones.
From your tehnicolor multigreen world
see me now
exiled Indian princess whom only you and the Nahuatl gods
                                        recognize
walking cold and dissatisfied but always straight and proud.

Well, I have repainted the primitive palette,
reversed the negative:
hair to one-color, Clairol Dark Brown,
blended my red and black nose into that paleface
with Revlon Demi-Rachel,
flattened my floppy tanned belly in silky tights
and caged my big tanned breasts in a double nylon holster

and write my songs to you
not freely like music
in smoke wind surf rain

but struggle newly with exact meanings,
then wonder if I have said exactly what I mean
on this clumsy electric machine.

Only my skin remembers that sun

I have carried that sun in my skin 3,000 miles
to find I have brought back a savage.
Firmly I inform it it is no longer subject to the small cloth it wore.
I muffle it in the wools and furs it has forgotten.
Reproachfully my cream brown belly looks out
                              between herringbone and knit.

In these short dark new days I am lost in seeking and earning
the wool the tweed the oil the quilt the double window and
                              the sturdy fence.
I play the fierce strong good tribesman in the hostile land.
I survive too well and every day it is harder to
                              remember that sun.

But at night the savage returns in the mirror,
reminds me that that sun has colored me back to
                              my primordial self
twenty great-grandpeople away
so the plane was more than place-to-place as flight information
                              would have me believe,
more the metal cone of some time machine
that in hours flew me centuries out of that jungle in
                              this prehistoric skin.

Now as the days and the savage fade I am less who I am.
The beautiful savage does not understand
but trapped in this time, muffled in this dark,
                              hidden from that sun
I am dogged and brave
and only my skin remembers that sun.

NY Times weather forecast, February

"Wed. and Thurs: The jet-stream
will bring snow to
the interior northeast
and a wintry mix
close to the coast."
Today we are in the city
close to the coast
so the wintry mix
may rattle our windows

while we envision up at the house
in the interior northeast
the snow the jetstream has brought
that covers the road the woods the roof
and our world is white, white
a tabula rasa on which to
imprint our lives.

"Southern Florida will be partly sunny
and warm, best in the Keys."
Wait for us warmly, Key West;
next week we'll be
in our café under the trees.

"Light rain will begin in Georgia" and I remember
the green, green kudzu covering the world,
and us, drifting in and out of sleep
on the futon in a jerrybilt newsouth house
listening listening to the rain and the jazz:
"A rainy night in Georgia..."

"Dim sunshine will be seen
throughout the Ohio Valley" and I am walking
across the vast campus
in my secondhand shoes
young and brave in the wet biting cold

dreaming of a good gas heater
that my landlady may install
in my old fireplace
or that spring will be early.

"Winds from the east will promote
sunny skies from Utah to Arizona"
and I think of my folding chair in the desert brush
the warm caress blowing by
and the Indian name I gave myself:
Sits in Hot Desert Wind and Drinks Seltzer.

"In Frankfort, it is 40/28,
In SanFran 63/50 PC (partly cloudy)"
but I don't have time to go today.

Every day I read that NY Times poetry and go
to my destinations, infinite combinations
of place and person and atmosphere
as I, in my chair, stay here
go there, live everywhere.

If I were a fish

The label the lady pasted on the package
says Scrod/Cod fresh from North Atlantic waters
and I think of the fish swimming free in the fresh
                                    North Atlantic,
what do they mean, Cape Cod? Cornwall? Iceland?
Where did my fish swim
before he died for me?

The second package says
Fresh Catfish Fillet US Grade A Farm-raised.
At first it sounds better to me.
He was given a brief, peaceful life
free of the huge North Atlantic waves
the pesky boats the voracious fishermen.
He lived in no peril
till his doom was delivered.

But I think if I were a fish
I'd prefer the waves and the danger.
My catfish was bred to be dead
but my scrod/cod
lived as we do, with choice and chance
and the illusion that he is free.

Acknowledgments

The Gypsy children. CONFRONTATION.

On passing my old office building on the Madison Avenue bus. CONFRONTATION.

Numbering the days. RAMBUNCTIOUS REVIEW.

Lost in Firenze. ONTHEBUS.

MacDump. THE NEW RENAISSANCE.

Futurcroots. DEKALB LITERARY ARTS JOURNAL.

The nursing home. ONTHEBUS.

Sunspot. ICARUS.

Only my skin remembers that sun. RAMBUNCTIOUS REVIEW.

I know the feeling. CAPRICE.

What I wanted to say. LACTUCA.

Winter morning. BRIGHT HILL PRESS ANTHOLOGY.

While recovering, I meet a lame pigeon. WOODSTOCK POETRY REVIEW.

The New York State Thruway. CAPE ROCK JOURNAL

Lunch hour in Central Park. WOODSTOCK POETRY REVIEW.

After you moved out of the upstairs apartment. POETRY NOW.

If I were a fish. CAPRICE.

GypsyGap. THE HIRAM POETRY REVIEW.

The symbol. CONFRONTATION.

Acknowledgments - continued

A small boat. DAN RIVER ANTHOLOGY.

Early stages. DAN RIVER ANTHOLOGY.

The calendar. ASPHODEL.

Flight 261. TIGER'S EYE.

Inheritance of stars. CONFRONTATION.

Six months after. CONFRONTATION.

Epitaph for the Twin Towers. IN LOVE UNITED, ANTHOLOGY

I pray to the god "Recycle". WONDER WRITING.

Losing it. CONFRONTATION.

The way machines die. CONFRONTATION.

Bio

Iris Litt is the author of an earlier book of poetry, WORD LOVE, published by Cosmic Trend Publications. She has had poems in many literary magazines (see Acknowledgments for a partial list) and has also had had many short stories and articles published. She has won many awards, including the ATLANTIC MONTHLY Award for College Writing, first prize in THE VIRTUAL PRESS short story contest, French Bread poetry award from PACIFIC COAST JOURNAL and others. She teaches writing workshops in Woodstock, NY, and has taught creative writing at Bard College, SUNY/Ulster, Writers in the Mountains, Educational Alliance, New York Public Library and many other venues in New York City and the Hudson Valley. She lives in Woodstock, NY and in New York City's Greenwich Village.

What I Wanted to Say
by Iris Litt

published by
SHIVASTAN Publishing
Shiv Mirabito
54E Tinker St. Woodstock,
New York 12498 USA
shiv@shivastan.com
www.shivastan.com

Printed in Kathmandu Nepal
Guru Purnima 2006

by
Mandala Graphics
sherap@nepalmandala.com

ISBN 0-9786484-0-4

SHIVASTAN Publications

Wildflowers: a Woodstock mountain poetry anthology, (13 great poets)
  Volumes I, II, III, IV, V, VI, VII available.

Woodstock Haiku & Anagrams: by Runly Acres

A Deep Blue Dreaming: by Richard J. Treitner

Night Travels to Tibet: by Marilyn Stablein

The Monkey Thief – Himalayan Tales by Marilyn Stablein

Welcome to Freaksville: by Shiv Mirabito (Foreword by Ed Sanders)

Maha Mela Bliss Trip & Other Poems: by Shiv Mirabito

Kumbha Mela Survival Guide: by Shiv Mirabito

Transcendental Tyger: by Shiv Mirabito

The Rythm of the Drums, Dreams & Nature: by Rosalyn Z. Clark

Confessions of an Artist: by Rosalyn Z. Clark

RASA or Knowledge of the Self – Essays on Indian Aesthetics:
  by Rene Daumal – translated by Louise Landes Levi

Ave A & 9th Street: by Louise Landes Levi

Towards Totality: by Henri Michaux – Translated by Louise Landes Levi

Whatever You Say May Be Held Against You: by Ira Cohen

Stanzas for Social Change: by Ed Sanders

This Book is for the Person I Love: by Christina Starobin

Atlantis Manifesto: by Peter Lamborn Wilson

Songs of Bo Baba: translated by Andy Clausen

The Walker: by Janine Pommy Vega

Breathe: by India Radfar

Cecil: by Rene Ricard

Original Presence: by Laynie Browne

Ceremonies of the Gong World: by Anne Waldman

SHIVASTAN Publications

Festival of Squares: by Andy Clausen (intro by Allen Ginsberg)

SAINTE-TERRE or The White Stone: by Robert Kelly

What I Wanted to Say: by Iris Litt

Where is the Woman?: by Enid Dame

Operation Minotaur: Photos by Indra Tamang
                        Haikus by Charles Henri Ford

BROADSIDES

Cecil: by Rene Ricard

Allen Ginsberg Dying: by Lawrence Ferlinghetti

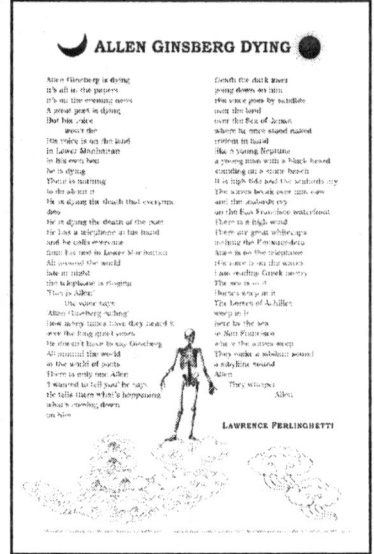

For further information about
SHIVASTAN Publishing chapbooks and broadsides
contact Shiv Mirabito at shiv@shivastan.com
or visit us at **www.shivastan.com**